Mandala
COLOR BY NUMBERS

Mandala COLOR BY NUMBERS

David Woodroffe

ARCTURUS

ARCTURUS

This edition published in 2022 by Arcturus Publishing Limited
26/27 Bickels Yard, 151–153 Bermondsey Street,
London SE1 3HA

Copyright © Arcturus Holdings Limited

All rights reserved. No part of this publication may be reproduced, stored in a retrieval system, or transmitted, in any form or by any means, electronic, mechanical, photocopying, recording, or otherwise, without prior written permission in accordance with the provisions of the Copyright Act 1956 (as amended). Any person or persons who do any unauthorized act in relation to this publication may be liable to criminal prosecution and civil claims for damages.

ISBN: 978-1-3988-1247-5
CH010165NT
Supplier 29, Date 0722, PI 00001992

Printed in China

Introduction

Mandalas have been used for thousands of years, most usually to represent a sense of wholeness and the composition of life, but nowadays, they are often seen as symbolizing the universe.

A Sanskrit word, the mandala is commonly associated with the ancient religions of the east. However, mandala designs can also be found in both ancient Mesoamerican archaeological sites and Christian church architecture. Over the years, their intricate designs have influenced artists, designers, and thinkers. For example, the psychologist Carl Jung would regularly draw small mandala designs to represent his feelings and state of mind.

This collection contains more than 60 mandalas. Some follow quite traditional design rules, while others develop the scope of mandalas in very different ways. All of them offer the coloring enthusiast hours of pleasure as they complete these beautiful patterns. All you have to do is follow the color key that can be found inside the back flap of this book. Alternatively, you can use your own selection of colors as you wish.

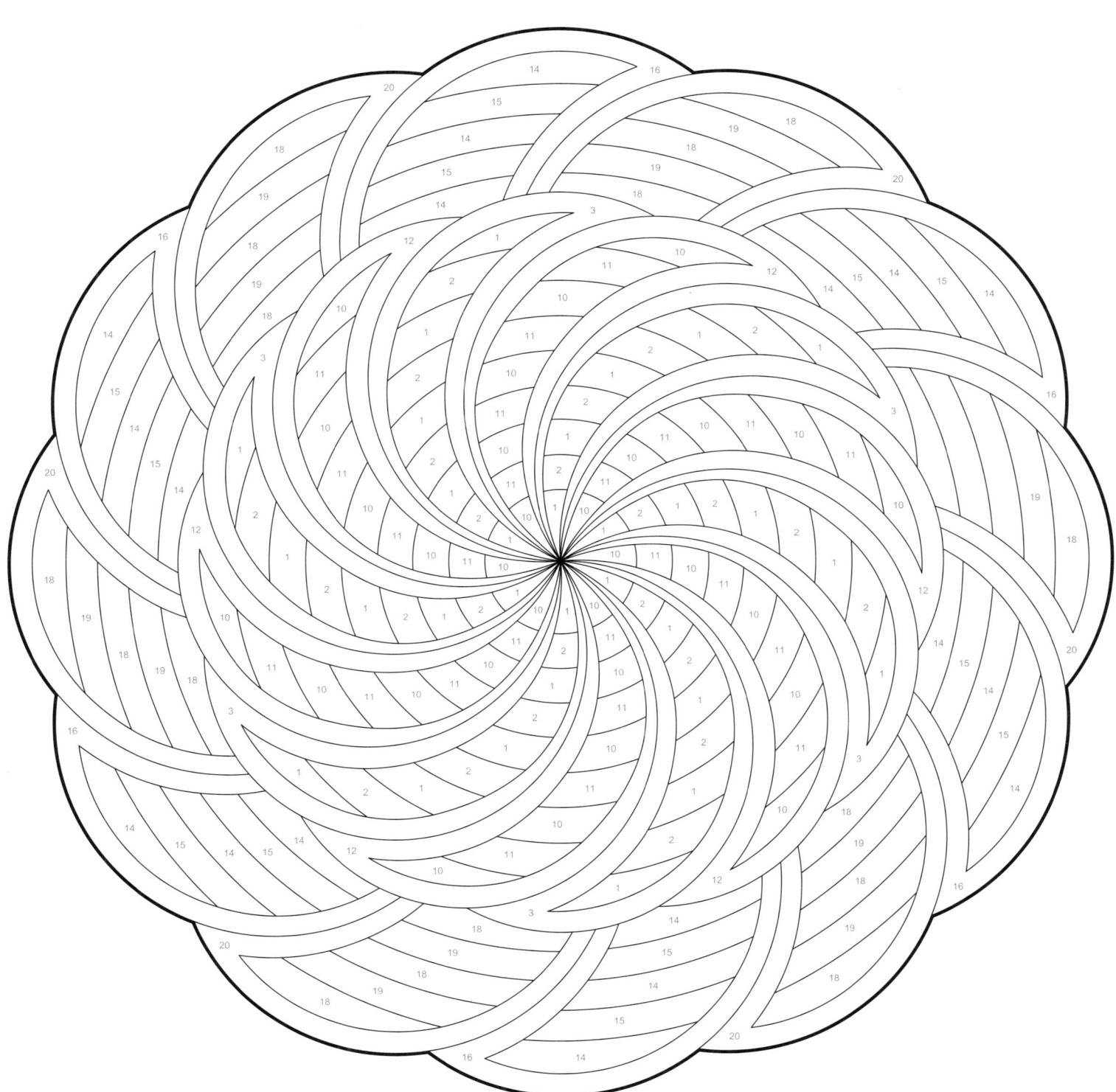

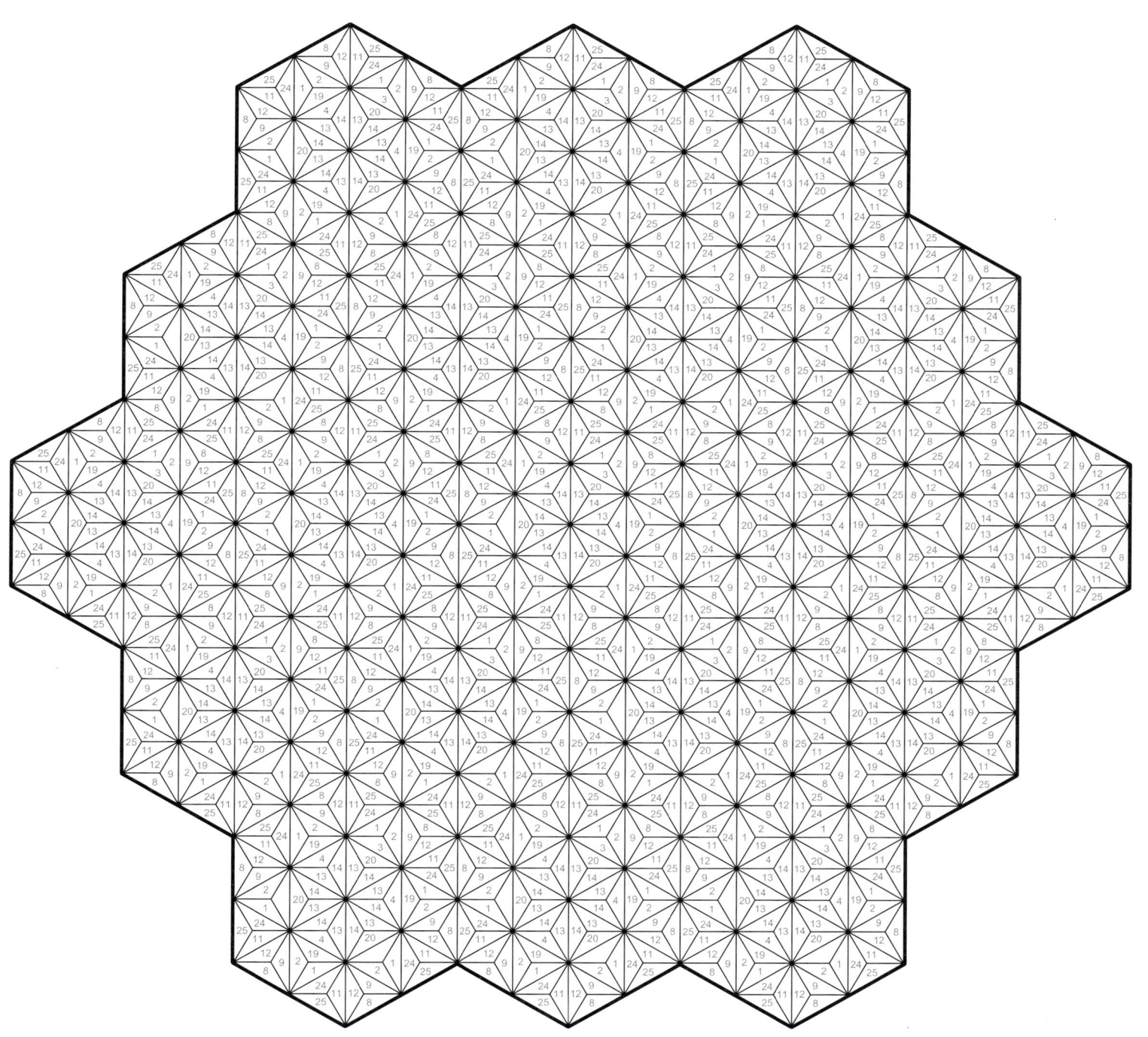

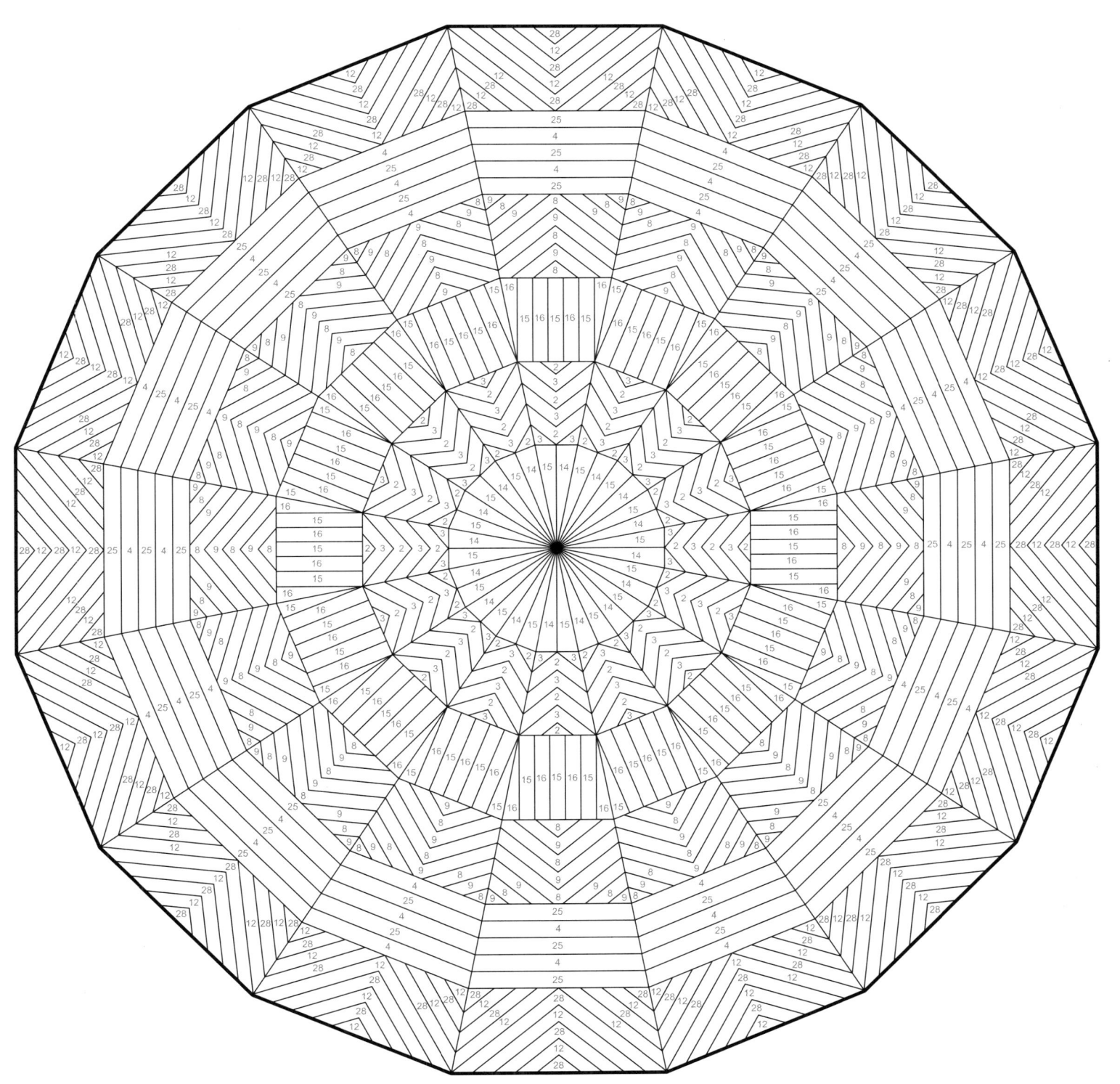

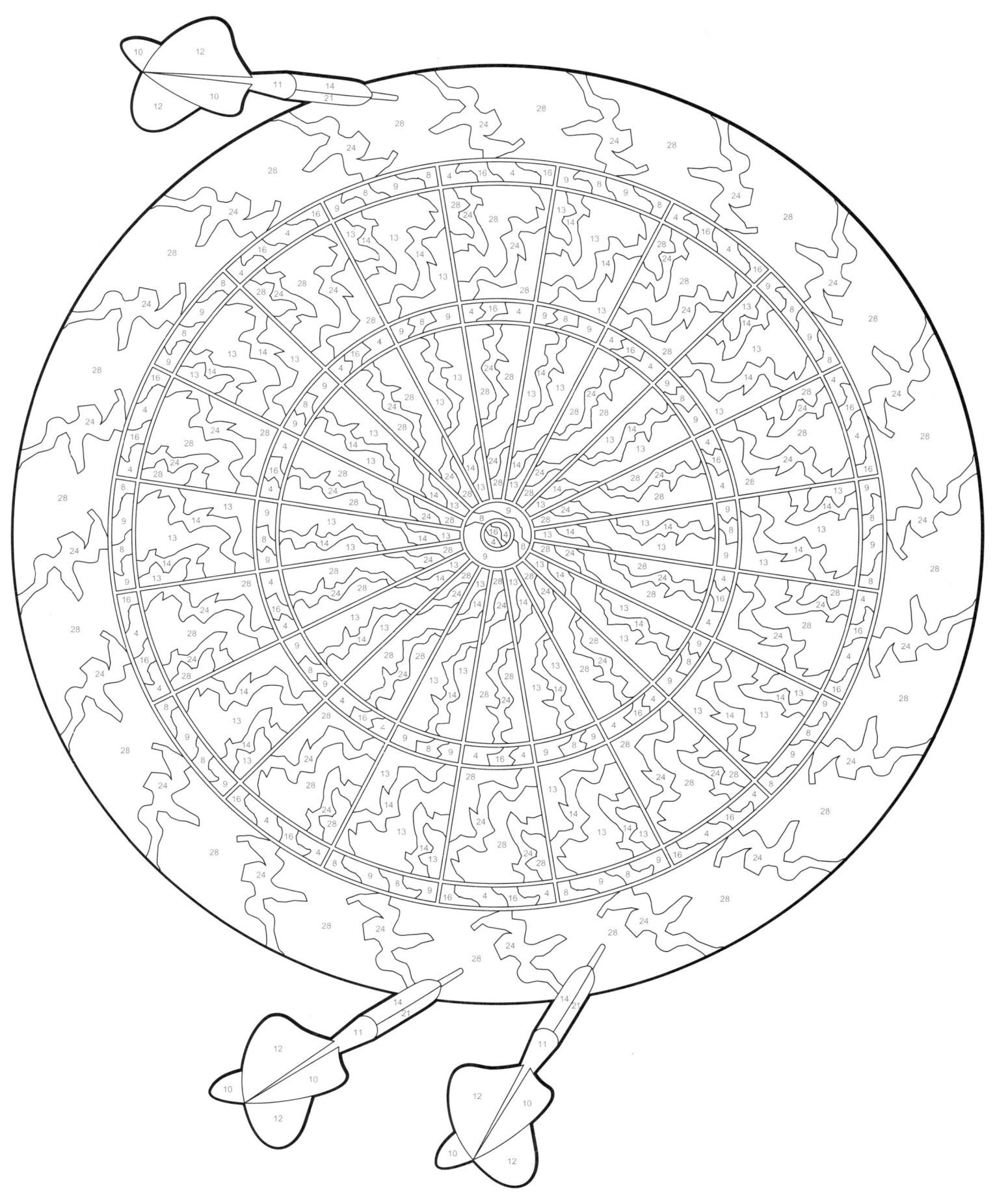

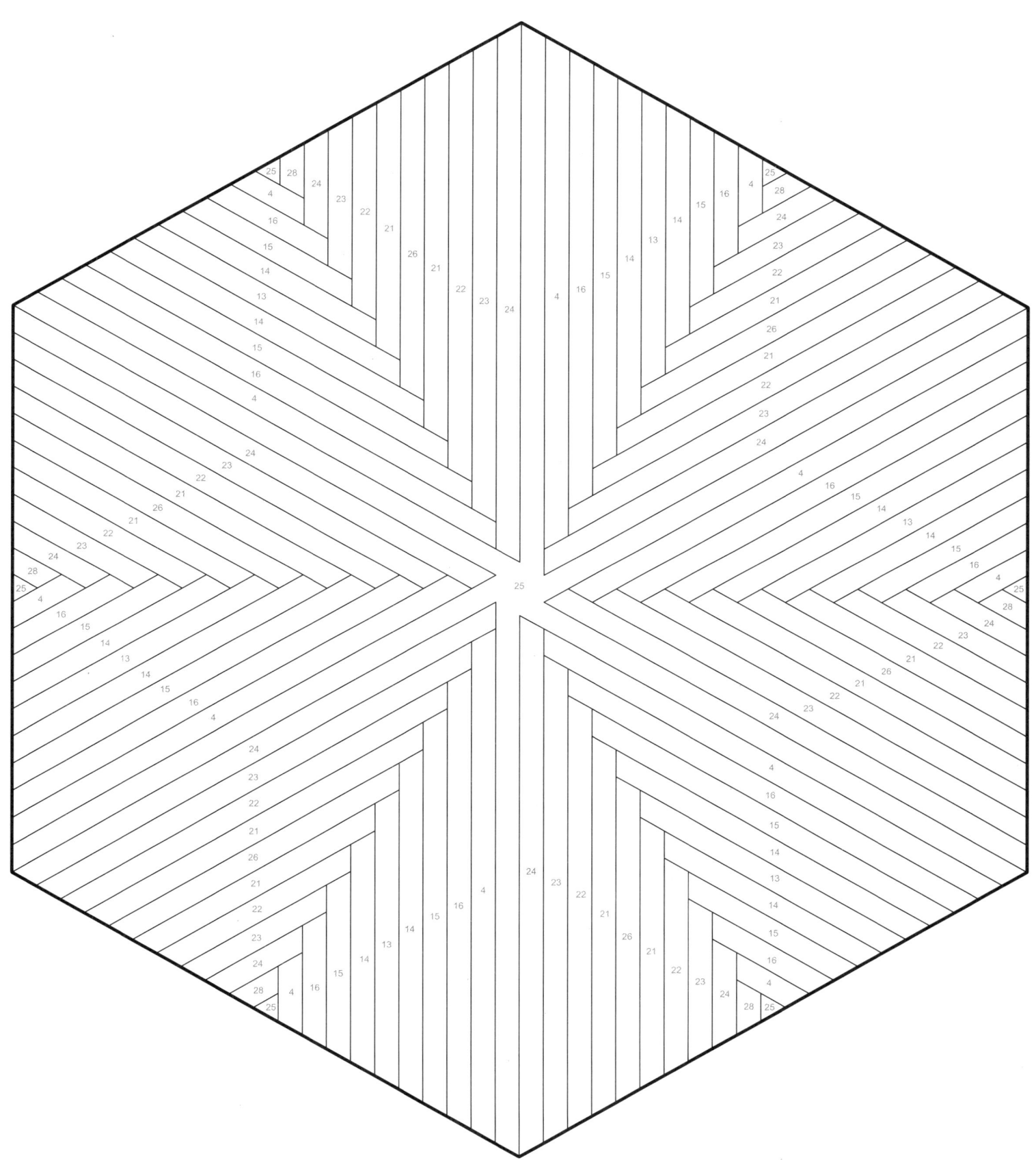

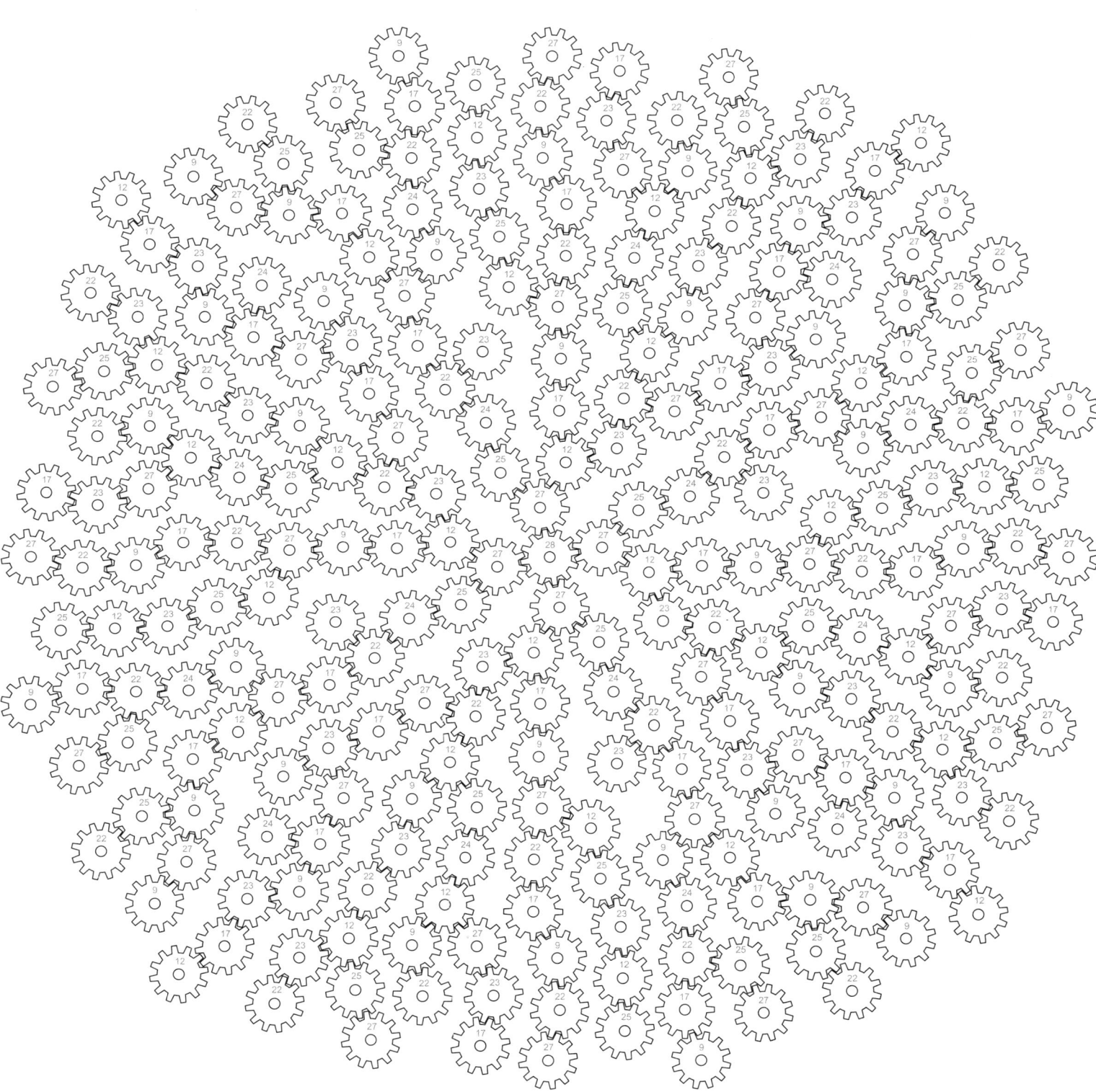

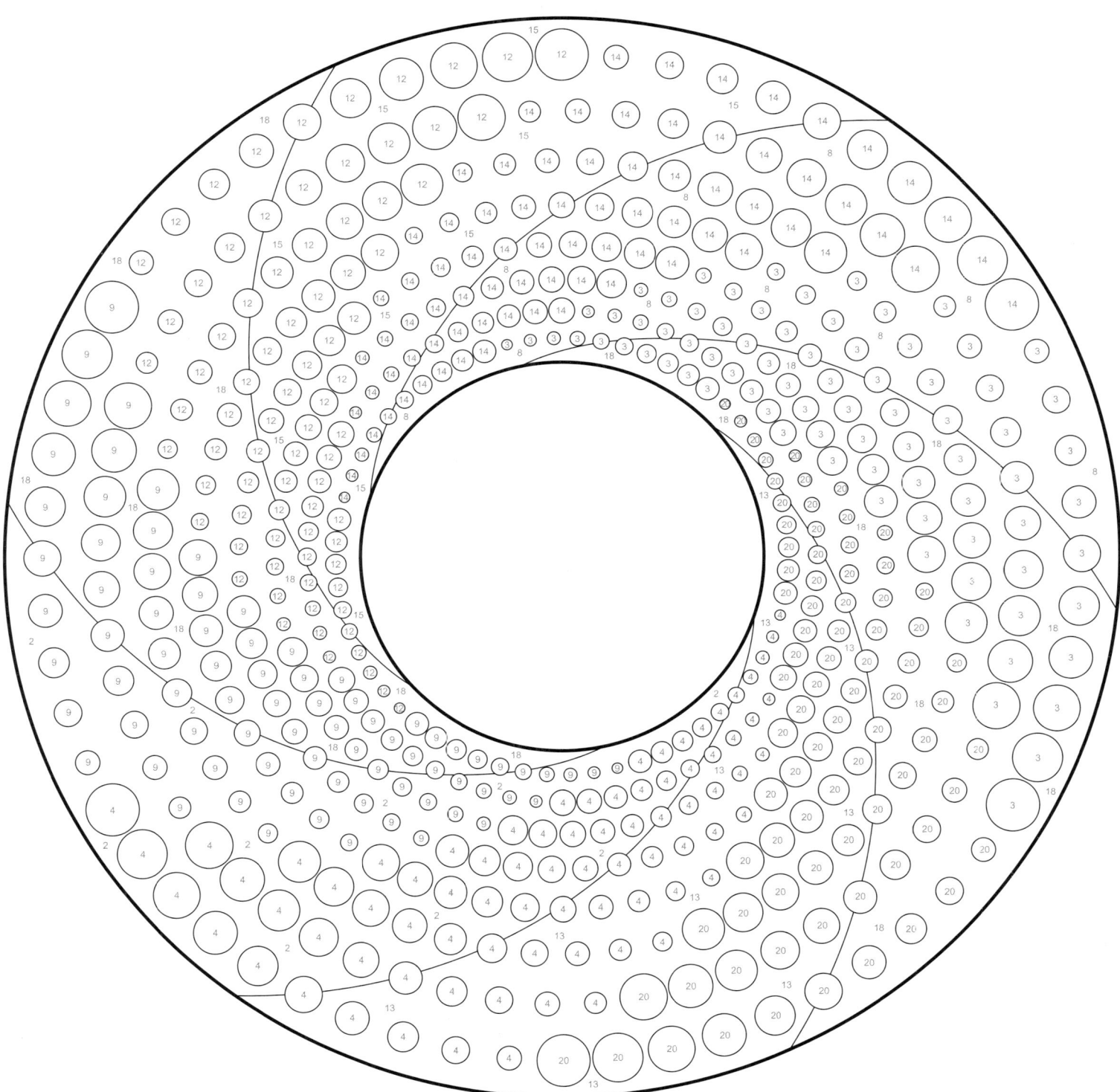

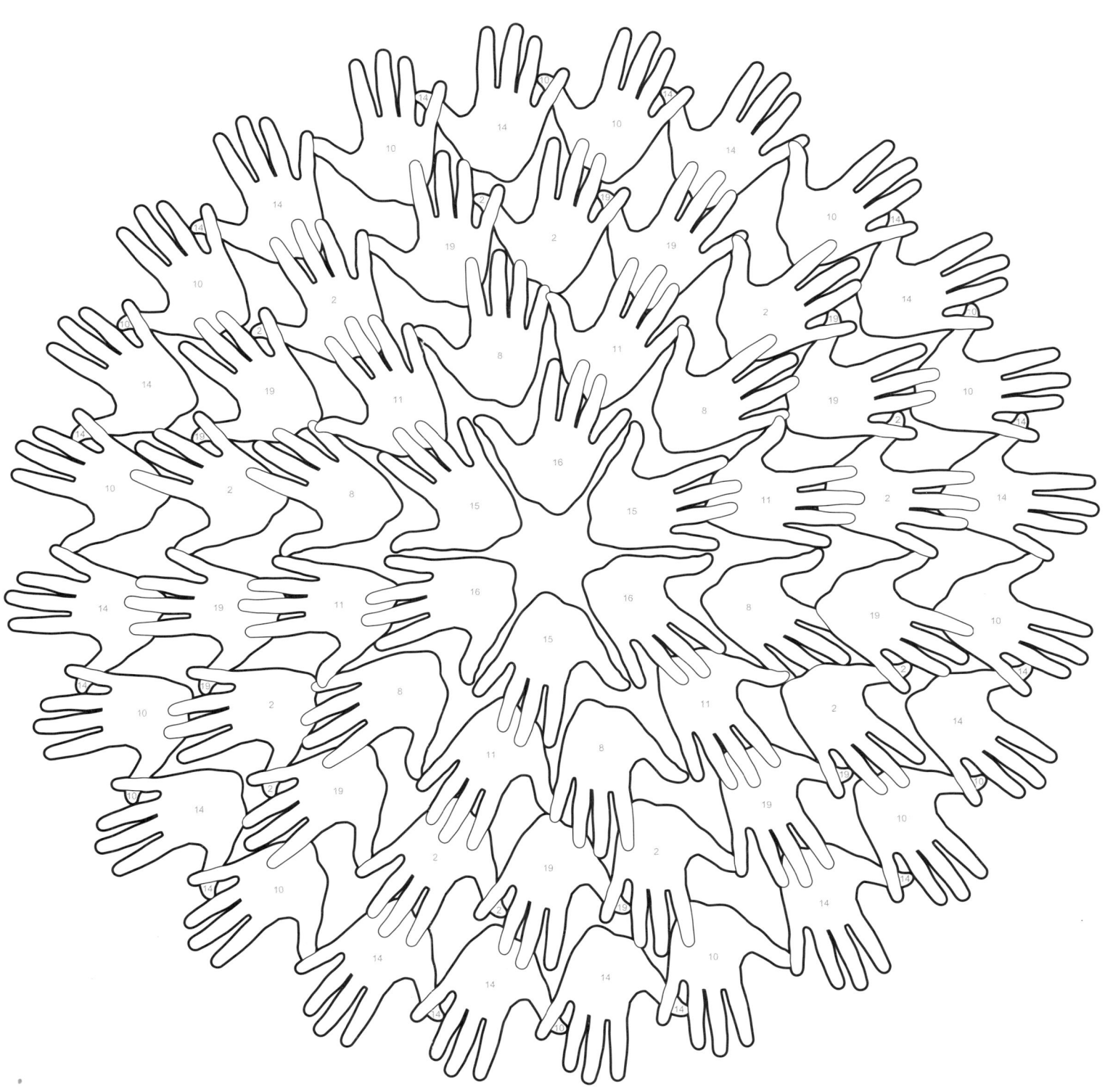

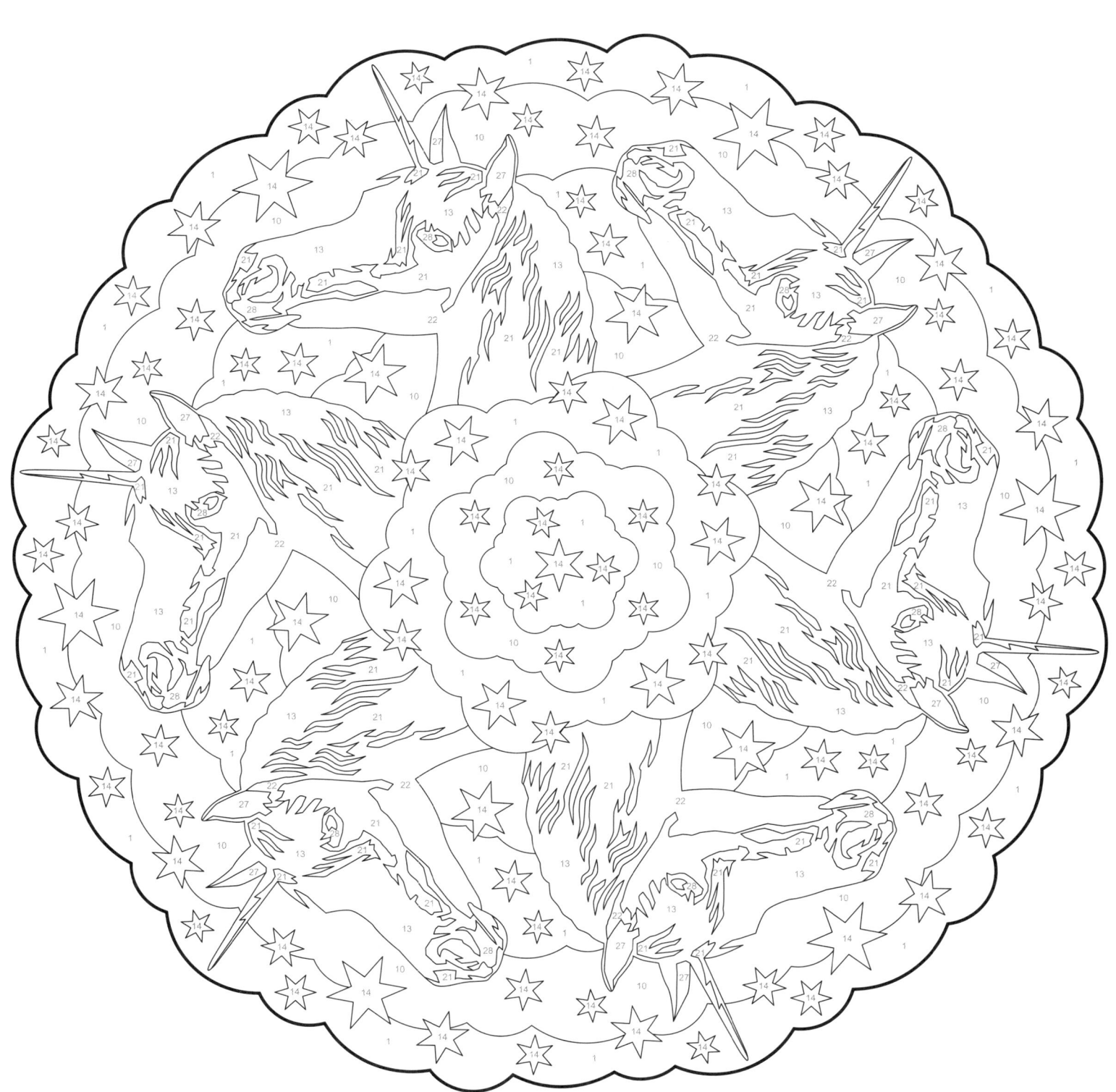

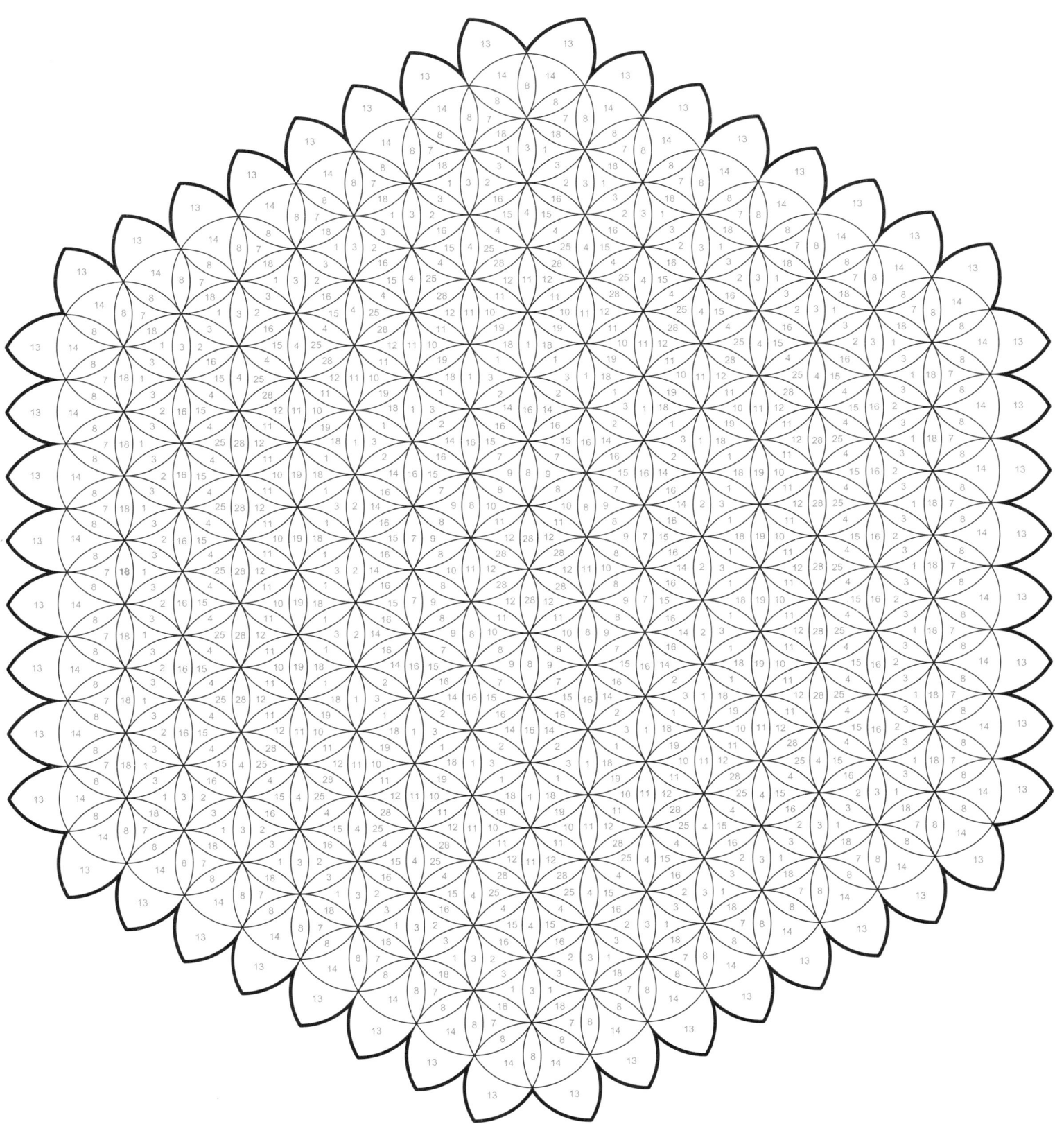

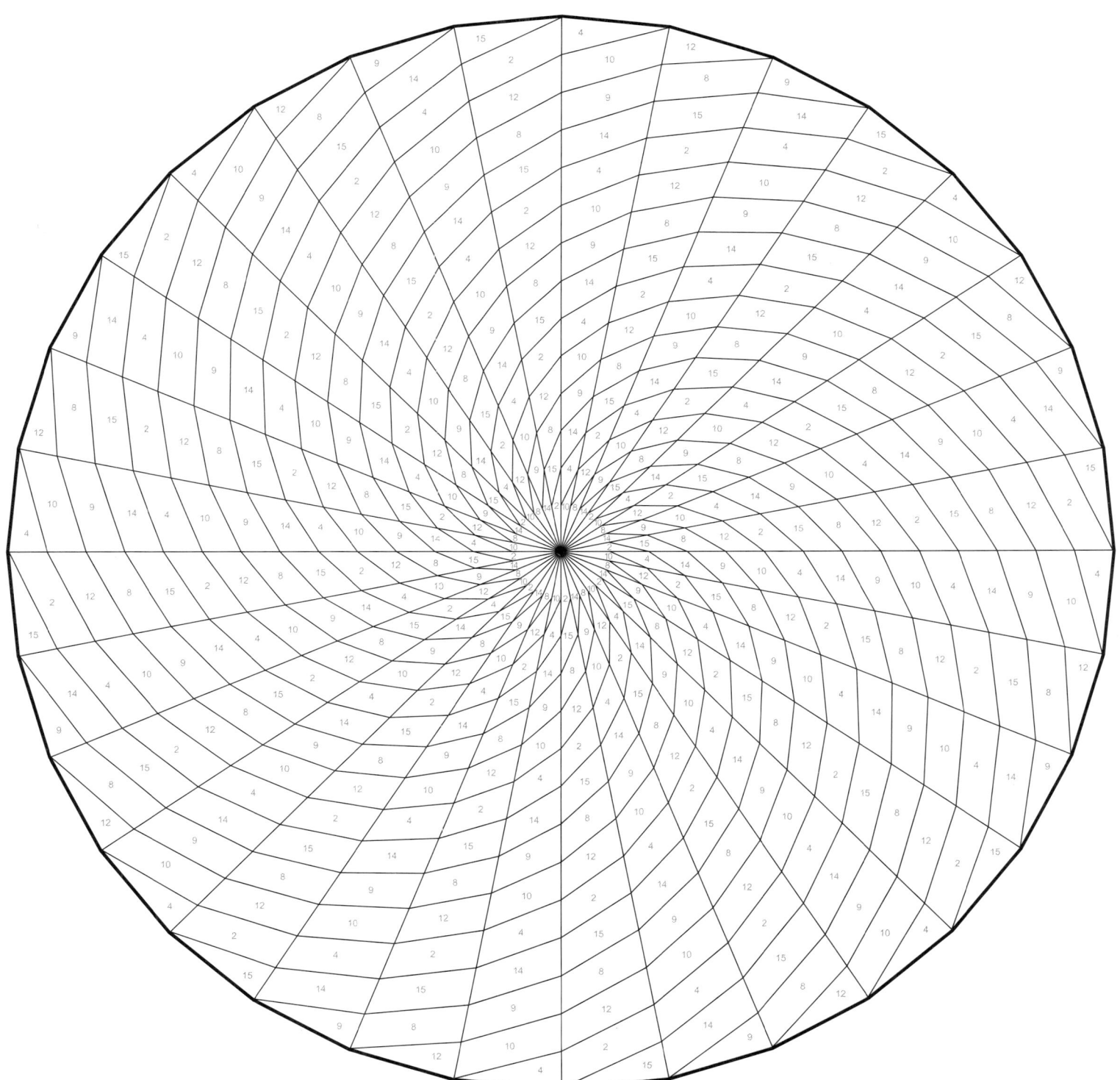

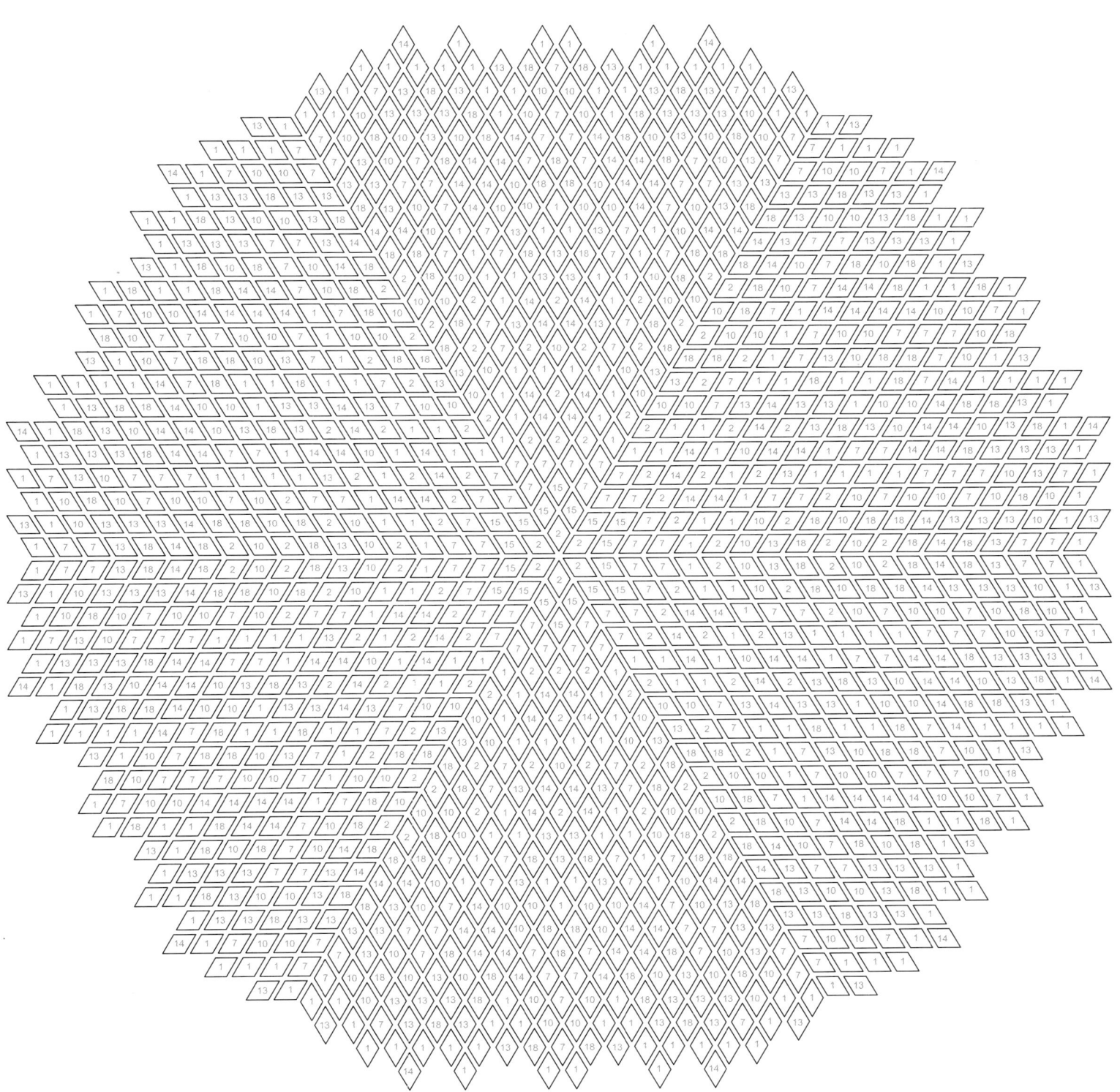